The Blackberry Domino

Taz Weysweete'

Wider Perspectives Publishing , 2021, Hampton Roads, Va.

© Jan. 2021 Wider Perspectives Publishing, Tasia Linton, Portsmouth, Va.
Taz Weysweete', the Blackberry Domino
ISBN: 978-1-952773-30-3

Dedication

It shook the planet of Norfolk to its knees
As some of the worst of us, always knew it would
Never heard the roar of emptiness until
Bad haiku after bad haiku was posted,
And you weren't there to call them out
That's when it hit me
You were really gone
I think now,
Who's an asshole enough to correct them?
—- All they gotta do is apply an element of nature.
((Goddamn))
But you're gone
So some write bad haiku or tell stories about you standing
humbly in their background while most of the chicks
reminisce like they regret not giving you the skins...

(Like, they could've made love to a whole legend)

I told you, you were a whole legend

Like, why can't you just break away from the shadows and
sit with me so we can talk shop about it?
I mean, I know why, but   I really expected more from
you.
No refurbished DeLorean?
Have you not figured out parallel universes?
Can we finally agree that science is fiction and you're
sitting with God somewhere picking his brain for the
perfect descriptions in the ultimate poem about how to
grieve your loss?

(don't laugh at me)

No?

I knew you'd say that.
And your voice will come to my eye ducts and pour over
my cheeks,
A stream of grain that tastes like salt and whispers like dust

On your birthday,
all they wanted to talk about was blood and bone
Quoting your pessimistic ass to the point of infringement
I don't even think You could've upset me more!
Last night
In the last scene
Of the last movie
I watched before I drifted off to sleep
The man died with his eyes wide open
His pupils dilated in the bright sky
(the blue shade, too familiar)
As if his tears were to water that last smile
And I hope you grinned
Maybe even let the phrase, "Holy Shit" lie beside you on
the pavement
I want you to know
I believe that you smiled
I pray it

Xo'

My Heart, thank you for every lesson

Jeff Hewitt
Legend

Contents

*Love me as I've always been. It's more than likely, that
this is who I've become.*

Pink Elixir

She smells like rose gold and nectar
Built as if someone had done Nebuchadnezzar one better

Eighth wonder of the world
lay her figure on her side
She becomes infinite
The innocence of her resurrection
lets you forget that
she died to get here

They will question her existence
Ask who built it
All while fondling her story, on pages, unabridged

Because they want her to be a lie
Because they want her to be the truth
Because they can smell her

Rose gold and Nectar

If a hummingbird is perched on top of a pyramid and no
one sees it…

Well, it sure tastes like God to me.

Bow & Arrow

Underneath an arrow of stars, a woman full of fire
combusts into a million snowflakes
returned to the earth
as if, she chooses to melt
as if, she wouldn't rather be ice
as if, she doesn't understand this day is short and the light
will be gone soon
as if, this won't seem like the longest night of the year
and it is
she needs the wind to split her lip
smear a crimson kiss across the moon
the mistletoe will be to blame
she needs to burn a path for the chariots that carry the
angels into her dreams.

Tracks

On cold train tracks, find warm bodies shuffling down a
path that leads to home
Remember the rage in the dog on the chain outside of the
tavern
The look in his eyes is sad, just as desolate as the girl
who's been pacing outside of that building all day
They both pray she finds a car to get in soon
Choking on a throat full of cum might be worse than
choking on a throat full of coke
But she'll take her chances
Buy the dog a bone with the change
Then hurry back to the tracks, because family understands

Been Gone Too Long

Been gone too long from the first form I longed to take over
But like a soldier home from war, my mind never really left the field
Still yield words like yellow lights, have to slow myself down when I recite it's like an eruption from the throat and my diaphragm is the volcano
Spit halos over heads, lay them dead. Looks like angels
Mangle metaphor and I punch lines two times the ass whoopin'
I still mic bang doe
One mic, word to Nas,
It's all I ever craved tho
like Pringles
Once I popped I couldn't stop
Like lays, I couldn't eat just one
Shit got so good to me I was hitting stages like
"I do this shit for fun".
Then I started feelin numb
Like maybe the lights outweighed the message
Like the crowd wasn't paying attention
Like I was saying real shit but since her man was in my face it wasn't connectin
Took my words to form and prayed behind page
Stuck to reading poems from the phone
So I wouldn't have to look you in the face
And say I'm not feeling it
Been gone too long from the first form I longed to take over

Weysweete'   5

Spoken word licks like a lover and my tongue is a cobra
My pen do pillow talk and my flow give cold shoulders
My rhymes like 69 and my loose-leaf a lady in the streets,
when I say these bars is tight it don't mean on the mic I
won't skeet
I gotta freak the bitch
Make the room go high pitch
I think I'm going back to work check the receipts
it's on documents
I does this shit
I just been gone to long from the first form that had me in
enraptured, my soul captured in sound, resounding from
my lips I forgot I was a wave
This what I do is not a phase.
It's everyday
It's my heart relayed using 26 letters in a thousand
combinations at a 100 miles an runnin, a conundrum in
the spotlight
Philosophy deciphered from the trap
Like if Marvin Gaye sang reggae and James Baldwin wrote
the raps
Like if Q-Tip taught Bob Marley to heel toe
A D Dot on Nayyirah Waheed tracks
A baby Narubi eating strawberry cookies learning poetry
from Mama Maya's lap
Like if Erykah Badu made Spike Lee the fourth pap and
they made me
A complete impossibility.
I stayed gone to long from the first form.
Back to the beginning.
Back to me.

Legend

(Dear Broken Woman Reprised)

Called my own self broken and they heard their names
I didn't call them broken
The third person was stronger than second opinion
Stronger than I
So I used him
Let the third person speak for me as if I had never parted
my lips on my own
As if my wrist doesn't twist this pen
As if all the heart breaks don't feel like the first
And the last
As if Eve doesn't laugh at what I am calling a woman
Broken
Not whole
As if it didn't take a whole bitch to convince man to put
some drawers on
And pull his britches up
The gig is up
A Maltese puzzle piece found buried in this temple of me
reads
Don't cry
You are not simple
You are sacred math
You are fire and brimstone
You are palm tree on deserted beach
Heaven becomes you
White sandpaper skin on the bottom of bloodied feet
Leave your mark

Let the sidewalks tame you
Into straight line
You are bow and arrow
No
I am bow and arrow
The third person
And second opinion have no say in that
I am bow and arrow
I hit targets depending on how the wind blows
A point and no direction
Broken and still perfection
Ugly cake at the checkout counter
You wish you had an extra dollar
Hit me till I hollered but I came back a legend
I came back a spoon full of sugar
I came back Aphrodite
They found 10 wigs in my coffin, headphones a Polaroid
of my brother and I and a picture of my three seeds
The remnants of a beast
I am not broken
I am a whole lot of heart and nerves
I am a whole lot of ocean and earth
They heard their names
When I called myself broken
I called myself broken
And they heard their names
I called myself broken
And they wrote their names
I called myself broken
And they changed the words

I called myself broken and don't even remember the
words to that record
I called myself broken
I made broken, legend

Shudder

she took toots from a silver spoon

(that they all swore should've saved her)

lied as still as she could in the middle of her California
King and waited for the drain

swallowed the aftertaste like sewer water with a shudder
and a smile

licked her full, numb lips over and over

she could taste the salt
she could taste the relief
moved her tongue over her teeth

(she could taste the relief)

3:43 am

she has work tomorrow but she is signing Keisha's song
along with Spotify and rolling another doobie

Fuck that

Kendrick could write his whole next album about this
moment

she thought to think
but stopped
dropped another line on Black Keys

Indebted to Divinity 1

miniature progeny pushed through my womb to deliver
me

and I am grateful,

a handful of common sense and a bucket to piss in, I wish
them more than this, but they fuck with it

how could I not break it back for that? run endless laps for
that?
take a cat nap and get right back to that?

I love them.

I am not mother of the year or Queen of Chuck E Cheese

But I know my son plays video games in his sleep

I am not her best friend or her confidant

But I know exactly how my oldest thinks

I am not the carpool mom or the one that can always treat

But my daughter could adopt every friend she has in the
world. If they're in my house, they will eat

my three put up with me
and my long hours and need for immediate sleep
my studio sessions and out of town gigs

they have to be quiet when I'm trying to memorize,
they can't talk to me when I write

I am grateful
They should've dumped me a long time ago.

But they keep me.

Cedar Grove

I've left so many of my fingerprints on the city bus
windows, that if you were to go back and dust them you
would know more about me than I've ever said.

Becoming a woman at a dollar and fifty cents a fare, the
evidence of that meandering through boulevards I could
never forget that names of,

my memories vaulted in terminals after midnight.

I've stood at bus stops under street light and prayed with
a cigarette hanging from my lip like I was at sunrise
service for one.

There is so much God in these streets.

The saints wear badges from the yard and the angels
adorn scrubs

Purgatory is filled with aprons, and sunken eyes and
strollers and hustlers

Our codes as smudged and detoured as the routes we
chose

down for the ride and forever imprinted
like the graffiti on the sides of the trains at the port and
HRT buses

Like Rosetta Stone to the touch
Braille for the eyes that see but don't look.

My deliverance could never silence this testimony.

I learned how to become at a dollar fifty a fare.

Indebted to Divinity II

a progeny traveled through my womb and delivered me
grown woman in a child's heart
my eyes
only old enough
to believe that they will discover all of the newness of this
world as I once did, and see it in that light
that they might overcome the sadness revolution carries
on the tongue and know that I fight for them
because I have to
loving them is not choice or circumstance
because it is true
and imperfect
I have to
like free will is a spirit thing
offspring of thine own blood
living reflections
fed through cord, then hand
every breath they take in unison with every beat of my
heart
the swords they hold the only I fear
but I wear no armor
I am at their mercy
Indebted to their divinity
their beauty and their rawness
in this creation of life
as I know it

40 Dollars

Ten dollars of gas. A dub sack. A pack of roll up. A BC powder. And lil' cocktails from the corner store. Is forty dollars.

3 teenagers in the drive thru and one mom, ordering a 3-dollar bundle and a few combos. Is 40 dollars.

A loaf of bread. A box of cereal. A gallon of milk. A pack of meat, whether it be chicken or beef and a bag of potatoes, my nigga it's 40 dollars.

Do not insult her.

A mother can do a lot with them 2 missed Jacksons
So don't apologize
She ain't sorry
Can get to the next day, the next mistake, the next emergency.
And yeah, sometimes this urgency gets out of her hands
And she hands you her pride on a silver platter, when you ask her, will 40 dollars do
Because it can
It should
It has to

Let's review, Subscriptions for Sony PlayStation, Netflix, Hulu and Amazon Prime will run you 40 dollars.

A babysitter, on a night you took off for months ago, just to find yourself struggling to stay awake for, charged 40 dollars

The kids got the flu this week, the prescriptions ran 40 dollars

So she have to take it
Make it with these babies, and this car and this headache for four more days
Maybe lay with a man who swears he ain't tricking but makes mention that he'll do what he can if he got it
So she does what he asks and toots out that ass
sometimes she smiles afterward
They both get a happy ending
She gonna make it to work tomorrow
and her baby practice
and perhaps this ho is hard to notice in the daytime
You respect her a little more with that 9 to 5 & her skirt down
You forgot that woman you call a whore was somebody's mother, didn't you ?
Just had one of those clear view flashbacks of that fake ass uncle Jack that would pat you on the head and slide his greedy hands to the small of yo Mama's back when he handed her 40 dollars
We don't need no scholars here
This ain't rocket science
Grandma always said it ain't what you do but how you do it

Say she remembers cooking dinners and selling them at
the speakeasy
Stockings cut off and tied at the knee
Said letting them get fresh with you, is how you kept your
profit
Don't matter how greasy his hair is or how slick the skin
Grin and keep yo' eyes closed

I don't suppose they called the elder women thots
More like, give them props for making it happen and
walking into church that Sunday
Their hats on high
Their children fed
Their drunken men found sober in empty houses
disheveled because the rents been paid

If God be a woman I bet that bitch keep her nails done
I bet she will her children feet clean
I bet she tell you don't worry 'bout what Jesus doing, like,
baby girl Peter and Paul on the scene
Bet you she prays for the girl who can't feel her knees

Shotgun at her head
Noose around her wallet
The price of pussy, cheaper than the fans from the funeral
home.
Niggas posting memes about her evenings while she clicks
"like" cause tears don't make noise
Them tears ain't sad no way
Don't make no difference how it got it done.

But know that 40 dollars didn't, even if it did save the day
God just got one.

Get fuckin for real

40 dollars?

I Saw Red, Not Purple

I didn't think Celie and Sophia woulda did Mary like that.

Nah, 'cause Sophia know what it like to defend yourself
and no one listen.
Steal away all ya life. Bring u back numb.

And Celie. Y'all see how she look at Shug.

She understand.

Why they let Mister do Mary like that?

T.R.O.Y. (abridged)

The weight of the world fell on the shoulders of a skinny
nigga whose skin was burned by a relentless sun, a sun
whose refuge is a body filled with tormented blood,
smeared slowly across the surface of the Earth,
but she moves
like paint races to dry and you muthafuckers just gotta
poke a finger in it
I've seen beginnings crash land into memories to get
drunk over
Found sober thoughts, while contorted in a position that
blurs the foundation of love
Salivating salvation and salutations, like sad love songs
that skip
But I'm a finish it if you look me in the eye and wipe the
tears away
Some day she will find glory in a kiss planted on her skin
where the aloe should go and find herself healed

You can't imagine what that God do for the blood

T.R.O.Y.

I've seen beginnings crash land into memories to get
drunk over
Found sober thoughts, while contorted in a position that
blurs the foundation of love
Salivating salvation and salutations, like sad love songs
that skip
But I remember dragonflies and honeysuckle in the
summer time, remember line for line Big Poppa and Can't
you see,
To this day, will ugly cry to that episode of Fresh Prince
when Will screamed, "why he don't want me man"
remember my first slow dance under a street lamp,
cobblestone under our feet and so much love in those
kisses
I remember house parties and watching fights go down in
the middle of the street, I remember I wrote poetry on the
front porch and raps down the block.
I remember I had best friends. I remember my mother's
laugh; I remember her crying over my stepdad when he
left. His bid ended 1 year and 3 months after she died. No
lie. I remember the day he told me to cross my fingers. I
remember how my brother danced, like the old Chris
Brown and that's any version, Michael Jackson. Usher
could never. His sister, his keeper. I am his biggest fan. I
remember his smile before the summer that broke it.
They say she died on impact
He and I died from the impact.
Remember when I had to tell him that, that summer

He dropped to his knees
B don't smile like he used to
I remember my rosaries
I remember the words
I never said them when I was homeless,
Or afraid, staring at ceilings and catching diseases
Figured God didn't need to see me like that
I remember getting my daughters back
I am grieving the lost time with my son
I remember the summers I thought would kill me.
My baby boy smiles like I am going to be a happy memory
in one of his summers
And I am grateful
Someday, I will find glory in a kiss planted on my skin
where aloe should go and find myself healed
I can only imagine what that God do for the blood

GT Baby
(From the Mud)

My soul all diaspora
all disaster
transatlantic backwash
and American cancers
no name ancestors and dignified captives
my blood line reactive
my life, target practice
my strife, been a habit
dark thoughts, a bit dramatic
my vibe can get traumatic
I've seen things
and I still gotta have it,
don't fear beings,
my soul all diaspora
all disaster
screamed massa into the stars one too many times
found oblivion in one too many highs
stood in one too many lines, on one too many dimes
got PTSD dimpled cheeks when I tell you I'm fine
maybe I'm too well behaved
my conscience a double edged sword,
the good and bad slave
lips pleading don't kill me, the body ready to die
born to run, and willing to hide
beaten
still kicking
ticking while time stand still.

My soul all diaspora all disaster
everything in me native
my mind spans
3 continents of homeland
a mesh of
honor and deceit
through rushing tears and clenched teeth.
My soul all diaspora
all disaster
a loaded gun
whispering the count to three
I always say a prayer
before I squeeze.

Poet

It's always a thing for me when I wonder on should I be
calling myself a poet.
Like, is this book poetry or prose?
The idea that I could be deeply felt
Quite possibly my only motivation.
The uncomfortable things that I say
The vulgar, the coy, the mean things that I say..
Get put out there and live
Next to the free and beautiful and the honest things that I
may say
I write to capture the duality of myself while it still exists.
I'm sure one day I will be whole
Leaving only my memory to cherish the debris

When a man cries it will break your heart.
But when a man dies, I always think, it's because someone
broke his.

A Written Testimony

"I got numbers in my phone
That will never ring again..

I got texts in my phone
That'll never ping again."

I got memories that replay vividly
Like Sophia's dreams of Sicily
Silly me to think that we
Evolve to peace from casualty
War remains inside our blood
It's only over when we're above
The pain we caused and was caused to us
More than metaphor
Ash to ash
Dust to dust
Become star and moon and particle
Can't be consumed by man, or fool, or article
Body gone but soul remains
Pretty muthafucker, this spirit vain
This train of thought a rocket ship
Break atmosphere to talk my shit
Angels curse
And angels spit
God buss a Milly in the center of all of it

(I forgot my mother's number)

"I got numbers in my phone
That will never ring again

I got pictures in my phone"

(Me and Cuh don't have one)

Carry out laws
Don't cry
We don't believe in karma wholly
But we are defined by loyalty
Holding
We bound
To supposition and making moves
We choose
How the days end
In Days Inns, kick in the door
Catch a Boss with a four for four
And a bad bitch
Maybe a snitch in his midst
Time will tell but we'll never know
First snow
Is where the hustlers' born
First day of Summer
When the soldiers are mourned
Pay homage in white tees and fresh ones

"I got numbers in my phone
That will never ring again
I got texts in my phone

The Blackberry Domino

That will never ping again
I got numbers
I got
Well
Sleep, well "

Stowe Water

Beloved,
born from my mind but I believe you ripped me
now I speak through the stitching across my lips
wish I could make you feel the deepest part of my
screams.

(I know you're leaving)

My chest left heaving as you chase destiny to the river.

She always wins,

but you run like the wind rushing through your hair will
lift you up and carry you across the water.

Make them say, "you seen that nigga try to swim ."
Make them say, "bet you a nickel that boy won't make it."

(but I know you're leaving)

The rapids won't outrun your spirit, your body snatched
down by an undercurrent who's only goal was to reclaim
Hell.

You died with your eyes wide open and your soul
drooling from the jaw.

I pray that you are brought back to me
so that I can wrap your skin in cloth
and make sure that you get home

Father Before Last

He uses
his hands…
his heart
to make them whole again
to mold a soul from skin
drained of life
so that a mother can leave the casket open
and it not break her granddaughter's heart
so that a wife can see her husband how she saw him that
first time
before this

He uses his hands
to straighten a son's tie for the last time , to clean that boy
up nice
uses his hands to
fill the man's chest up
to lift his chin
to close his eyes
uses his heart to lift him up high, treads mind for psalm
to explain an old pain to new survivors
every word drenched in fresh dirt and roses

Tight Like Jada and Pac
(For Chocolate Chip)

I remember how much I miss you in a sharp breath that
pulls from a space underneath my rib

You were once my protector,

A muthafuckin' instigator, as if from incubator, you'd
been talking shit

I loved that

Because most everyone only pretended to. Drawn to you
because I could see the lie in your eye.
I spoke, because I was daring you to try me.

You never tried me.

Not my body, not my trust.

The morning they told me that the car you were in
wrapped around a light pole after a high speed car chase
down the interstate

I went numb
Felt cold
(I didn't react)

They say almost everything broke on you

Taz

(they don't say everything broke in you, but it did)

I'm not better than you
I'm not better than you
I'm not better than you

But I can't look you in your eyes sometimes
Don't know if I am watching reflection or prisoner

Don't know how to love all of the darkness without trying
to shake it out of you

(bitches can't keep their hands to themselves)

Don't know how to love all of the darkness without trying
to shake it out of you

(I ain't yo bitch, but give me a bump)

I can sit here for a few
Crush candy rocks down into flavored straws and break
flowers down into smoking gardens

And we can pretend that this is as pretty as that sounded

As you look at me in a way that lets me know it will never
be the same , but this is what we got now

Missing you to your face
Because I love you like that

Tell the Mothers

Remember to tell the mothers that heaven is beautiful,
remind them of walls covered in ivy and gold the smell of
lavender and lilacs and chicken fried on a gas stove.
Their son will eat good at the table.
Whisper he is forgiven in her ear and pray to God in
apologies. Don't look her in the eye when you kiss her
cheek. That is still her son's job. Hand her a dish towel
and let her pat her own face dry of tears and sweat while
she beats steaming potatoes like she is mashing his killers
face to death in a pot she can control.

For whom the bell tolls is why she weeps
'Cause murders like these happen every week
And my brother just died like this had happened before
I can't make sense of him not being here no more
Somebody come tell the mothers that heaven is beautiful.
Shit, somebody come tell the whores.
Tell the fathers.
Tell the pimps.
Tell the trappers
Tell the fiends.
Tell the church.
Tell the baby mama's and the niggas with jobs
Tell me.
Tell the law.
Remind us of walls covered in ivy and gold and the scent
of lavender and lilacs and chicken fried on a gas stove.
Our son will eat good at the table. Whisper he is forgiven

Taz

in her ear and pray to God in apologies. Don't you look her in the eye when you kiss her cheek. That is still my cousin's job.

The man that killed him was found.

Tell her that Twin is laughing, serving hand to hands over walls covered in ivy and gold.

His baby mama still in that car.

But tell her, he riding big now the smell of blood vanished into lilac and lavender.

His mama ain't doing no more interviews.

She don't wanna hear shit but the poppin' of grease in a kitchen built to serve her King.
Tell her they frying chicken, rolling reefer and sipping tron' all up in through the kingdom. Tell her that boy''s belly is full. He paid for that seat at the table.
Tell His Children He Sent It In

Whisper he is forgiven in their ears and pray to God in apologies.

Know that he won't become the
old man
with cloudy blue eyes
and the bald head
that listens for his Maker in the dark

where worry exists
but Faith makes room
but somehow was consumed with enough life that he left
each of us a piece.

And when she faces you with her entire soul on her
tongue and asks you when he'll be home, you make sure
to hold that woman by the heart and speak through the
flood rushing down your face. Don't let your voice shake,
and you tell her that heaven is beautiful...

He And Her Savior was never scared

Poppa O.G.

The world is ending,
like you did.
All of a sudden and I'm wonderin'
if this is you,
burning the muthafucker down.

The world is ending,
just like you did, all of a sudden
and I'm wonderin'
if this is you
burning the muthafucker down.

The Blackberry Domino

Some dope shit about resurrection/survival

1982

transfixed in parallel universe
I step off of the curb on my tippy toes
thinking
everything we ever imagined would happen
did
with the exception of teleportation or flying cars
(like, Keurig's freak me out, ya dig)
and,
I mean
it's strange to even debate this particular "I told you so"
because in one way or another we knew
well, with the exception of the dying
there has been so much dying
I mean,
but we knew there would be dying
we just didn't know who
or how close they would be
or how much of my air that they might take up in a day
I lose my breath when I speak their names
comes out in whisper
or tear
sometimes like an "I told you so"
that only makes dog bark
still
everything we ever imagined would happen
did

Taz

the Civil War
the South rising
the world leaving us to it.
I am thinking
        where are there still carousels?
I'd like for my father to get me a pony,
I am thinking
that is all I remember of him
and how to tie my shoe, my mother taught me, but he was
in the room ..
everything we ever imagined would happen
did
except for everything after that
the words buried
beneath the wilted petals of forget-me-nots
and cigar ash

Monarchs' Court

The Kings run in packs
Leave their tracks on trails covered with other men's
defeats
They post up in front of castles and cathedrals as if this
were cleared by both God and state
They negate the traffic that doesn't equate to any revenue
to down the street and so and so cut spenders deals that
they will die,
they live for their children and conquest
It's best to shy from their eyes

From Ma Dukes to Kings

he ain't never had much. he ain't never had nothing.
but he can make you feel things.
his voice can reach down underneath your navel like he's
feeding you umbilically
his voice can pierce through your brain
you will hear his voice in your head and believe
you will hear his voice and know he knows your pain
it don't take much to give a Black man hope
something like giving a Jamaican some boats
something like a cat from Detroit calling his brothers and
their women a nation
something like traveling the world and taking death by
blood out of the equation
something like convincing us we are worthy of our own

he ain't never had much. he ain't never had nothing.
the mind is not limited to possession.
Fred Hampton saw Garvey's dream
Malcom deciphered what Fard left unseen
Aren't we living longer eating clean?
We know there won't be a school, but damned if we don't
understand what we need?
he ain't never had much. he ain't never had nothing.
Like, Bob or Baldwin or Eldridge or Jesus
he will leave for a while
hide inside of world's where his words still matter, where
they still believe
It don't take much to give the Black man hope

It don't take much to give a Black man a dream
But isn't it something what we do when we pull the
blueprint out of the scheme?
he ain't never had much. he ain't never really had nothing.
but when he opens his mouth.
God knows, I believe.

Kingdom

finds perfection in the sleepy eyes of his children.
finds peace in the restless soul of his woman.
finds loyalty in the steady breaths of his brothers.
finds himself grateful.

his joy is quiet.
his joy is home.

Bamboo

follicles filled with the old Atlantic's water,
roses will bloom from their kinks
leaves will sprout from their limbs
roots will settle
and spread
reach the core of the planet
the petals will burst like volcanos
from their eyes
the rain won't wilt them
the ice will protect them
this Earth will keep them
these buds
these boys
will grow
these men
will be flowers

<u>Ironbound and Longhill</u>

razors buzzing, necks on fire, tears in eyes
black men slumped low in easy chairs. The peace of a
reclaimed nap spread across their faces.
the young boys don't wanna be here
necks craned and fingers flying. Several different digitized
theme songs all going off in sync
do not leave out, Baby Shark coming out that one stroller.
Such and such baby mama was up in here the other day
They dragging her for filth. Apparently, that's her baby in
the stroller
Conversation in the air floating down on you like aerosol

"Air BnB's is the White man's version of a rooming house.
You can make some money."

"I think the government had something to do wit it. Put it
like this, the government aids the brainwash. Nigga was
brainwashed"

"That girl fuckin you, you the one in here with a stroller!"

And the choir of laughing sounds like joy on Sunday
morning.

One cut might take an hour and a half. Another man
might be here for two. Appointments pushed back into
catching up while the barber finishes. You don't rush
artists. Somebody will get sensitive about they shit.

Look at the mirrors. Look at the tattoos. They do this. They live this.

Wives checking up on husbands, bets being made.
Somebody comes through with wings, now the whole
shop ordering wings. Now, the whole shop talking shit.
The young boys sit up a little taller when such and such
walks in. The man with the CDs fixes cars, sells drinks and
fire sticks. Everybody need Unc.
Unc needs them, too.
So much respect in one room.
Head nods and daps.
Nobody fighting over who's been here longer.
You can tell ain't nobody in a rush to leave.
The door chimes, and here come such and such mama,
and the girl who sell bundles, and the girl who boost Pink.
And the girl who owe such and such ten dollars but she in
here beggin',
Cause she be beggin'.
PlayStation gets turned on by the owner's son ...
The radio gets turned up on 2 Chainz and Ariana...

I am watching a baby get his first cut, the barber done told
him chill out, "You ite" and the Lord knows he's
maneuvering that child.
And I just kinda smile.
These black men are safe here.

Taz

Immortal Combat

They wanna stone Shawn Corey Carter
Say, he wanna barter the revolution for a dollar

Say he just another figure head martyr we honor, cause he
came from the gutter

Another dope boy turned hustler who muscled his
mustards on to wall street

Spoken into existence, Fuck Jay-Z
Did you know the Kalief Browder story was co-produced
by Weinstein

Did you know he cheated on his wife?
Who don't know his wife is Beyonce

Did you know he never sat in court one day with Beans.

Shit, he wouldn't even give Dame the dough to fix his
teeth

They wanna bury Barry.

Say Barrack dropped bombs on babies burst like
blackberries in his fingertips

Signed one too many documents in blood

And oh, how he cooned I mean crooned those speeches,
like the gatekeepers aren't the puppet masters

8 years tap danced past us

And I gather,
Martin was a bad husband.
And Malcom was a bad husband.
And Nelson was probably a bad husband.

And I wonder if you think the revolution is up to man or
God?

Who dies when we don't win?

Aren't they just men being put up on a podiums that
somehow favor auction blocks,

As if, these men aren't lucky to have been chosen by
masters they outwitted

I mean the feds ain't no joke
They had Muhammad committed
Look how they did those beautiful black Panthers, how
they purged the purr of pride from those powerful felines
and murdered it on each set of their lips

Or is it God on that stage?

Was that the God who never returned a blow?

Taz

That God they locked away for 27 years.

Last time that I checked, was it God they shot down in Crenshaw

Is it God, who served fiends on nights to quiet the stomach grumblings

God who died holding a pack of skittles.

They wanna stone Shawn Corey Carter
They wanna bury Barry

And I wonder what a Black man has to do to be viewed as human

Eclipse

these fields

the plains just look golden to the boys who mow and hurl
pigskin, corral

to the boys who become men who take care of stock, and
herds and harvests

the men who send sons off to war, to make a name for
themselves in a world that honors those plains

these fields

the plains just look like clearing and blood and sacrifice

to the grandfathers of men who raise boys to never pick
and plead or run

to the men who will never bend at the waist or bleed from
the eyes,

these fields look like wasteland
like burial place
like circumstance

Taz

these fields
be neither playground nor workplace anymore

not to the man who stands a man

who stands, free

Time

minutes blur into years
seconds become decades
time is more rare than gold, fire is never-ending
the mending doesn't always happen
the forgotten don't owe you their memories or their
tomorrow… should it be one.
a stare that indicates how much you never cared before
he could've died half past the last time you thought about
him.
or wrote a letter.
or came to visit.
he doesn't know you don't have no money and you don't
look good.
he doesn't know you are getting high and lost the kids.
he doesn't know you lost yourself.

You don't write.

weeks became the first year
one day, you fucked another man.
the next day you lied.
he doesn't know that.
just that
he don't got nothing on his books
he hasn't talked to his mama in weeks
he's having flashbacks from when he got jumped in the
shower
he can't sleep

Taz

the forgotten don't owe you their memories, or their
tomorrow.
and there will be one.
we will remember.
starch filled skin, worn like biker jacket leather
fluoride filled thoughts and a hot Takis sex drive
bitches craving pen dick like, "yes daddy!
Give me all that sadness.
Fill me full of pain!"
Slain in your master's bedroom, each stroke to give him
his pride back.
creep to keep love to yourself
always selfish, even with you, don't you deserve more
than that?
he could've died half past the last time you thought about
him.
he doesn't owe you his memories.
you don't owe him reality.
you could've died two minutes before they opened the
cage.
Adam and Eve got stuck with each other in the same
fuckin' way.

*Do you think that
the stars war with the night's sky over dominion?
Or do you think that they've always known
that they belong together?*

The Welder

he left eight years of yesterdays on her skin
held her past midnight and asked her when was the last
time she'd smelled dawn?
when was the last time she let her soul drip from her eyes,
or spent the night on the other side of Hell
could she let herself, melt.

he had left 8,760 hours of kisses on her spine
it took him five minutes
she could recall them in the seconds they were planted
could feel them when the time moved, like how the
planets do its moons
Shifting inward eye, out of range
Resting in her palm.

most dreams end when you wake up.
the fairytale lifted like her eyebrow, all the while an unlit
cigarette between her fingertips, is subconsciously twirled.
an afterthought by dusk but still worth the time.
he comes back to her when the sun is out.
He whispers to her like the words will disappear if she
doesn't catch them
she lets him
remind her
of love

Taz

Spaniard

compulsive in the way I have loved them
more than once seemed real enough to claim
but men aren't new nations or waters
more river and mainland
found myself excited to discover what was already there
just as ignorant as any Columbus or Vespucci
giving another's home my name

1/2

If you see in me,
Who I believe you are
Without each other
We will never be whole

Taz

<u>Saints</u>

This one boy, when he kiss me, he put flowers in my cheeks.

This one boy, when I watch him leave, I get oceans in my eyes

This one boy, when he tell me 'no', my heart hears 'yes'

This one boy, I never knew, but I know when he was mine.

This one boy, I don't understand, but I scold him like I do.

And all of it is forever.

Every Adam

lost myself inside of the blackest face
one too many times
but really
all the atoms, at their foundation, are built the same
lead easily by my wanting
stray just as quick in my nonchalance to keep them close
I've been told,

that they didn't know that I cared…
       and I nod
because they know that I did
what lip service does that deserve?
wasted breaths on words they never hear
ain't even checking for
so instead
I fuck them up
by answering when they call
in the middle of the night
5:30 in the morning
maybe during their lunch
really, forever
so that they
can't ever forget
(don't you never forget)
losing one
like me

Sweet Tooth

Your name rests on the tip of my tongue
but never gets to taste my lips.
I make you kiss me before you go
so that I can leave my signature inside your mouth.
So that, maybe, my name will be the thing you crave at
night.

Miracles

I could explain heartbreak
in such a way
you'd fear love like I do.
But I would rather
write out my daydreams
in such a way
we always
believe.

Rebel Hours

I make love to him like I'm trying to make the paint melt
off of the walls and the floors curl
I try to drain him
I try to make him resurrect
I try to banish and elevate his name in the same breath
I've come close to death caught in his stares and I wish to
God I didn't feel him when I moved, the way he fills my
insides I am bursting from the outside in back insides out
everything throbbing
popping
Papi cause me metamorphosis
This nigga changed me
Rearranged my thinking and my blinking
Had me tweaking for dick and knowledge
Like a scholar with a stripper pole
Dipped in gold and covered with a sock
Knocks
Like when he used to drive that Mitsubishi and I would
creep him in my teepee
Believe me
He have you fuckin' like a thot
Non-stop
To trap songs
And top shelf on my breath
Giving him everything he make me feel back
Like I ain't got nothing left

<u>Eden</u>

make my mouth wet

pour pomegranate seeds wherever you'd like

make a garden out of me

make my mouth wet

diamond vision, think in prism,

he seen my reflection 104 full moons ago,
an infinity has passed

he is my tomorrow and yesterday at the bottom of a half
full glass

make my mouth wet

Taz

Around the Way

I will call you my baby, forever,   or something like it.
Don't mean I'm ya mama
Don't mean I'm your girl
But Imma call u my baby, forever,   or something like it.
Forgive me if I describe you pretty.
I'm not trying to deny the fight in your eyes, I just think it
floats like a butterfly
My baby, forever. Or something like it.
Don't mean I'm your mama.
Don't mean I'm your girl.
I can't raise you
But I will lift you up
I do not lie with you
But I will praise your name.
I'ma call you my baby, forever. Or something like that.
Please forgive me.
It comes naturally

Slow

she said softly,   sweetly
sounded siren.
surrendered seas.
salvation slipping
sinfully steeping
soul seeping seemingly smitten
shooting stars sans solar system

so slowly, sun slipped south
set
salivating
stirring
subtlety swept
suddenly spent
sweat shining

Succulent

savored wetness clasped
reveling in my puddles
and coming home soaked

<u>Equator</u>

The sound of crunching fruit in my ear, feels like love
down my spine
he talk with his mouth full
I listen with my face
my foot is in his lap
his heart is in his nose
just as red, as our bond in the open air
this kitchen table, our equator
the hottest spot on Earth

<u>Bane</u>

I think maybe
he knows exactly what he is doing
make
me
smile deeply
like the sun is being watered on my face
he know how to talk to me
let his words slip from tongue
like tide from shore
he tease
he's mean
(I've seen nightmares in eyes, wide awake)
he stroke me like tomcat
this, something else
this, not 'bout me
(we never take offense)
I should take offense
but I don't
he makes love in the morning
before the air hits his throat
to remind him
all there is
is my love

Play You

Our syncopation like symphony but it feels like unison
when you move, I move
and it's just like that
sheet music

an intrinsic sequence
foreign to the eyes, but I have felt this before

playing from my belly, with no control of my fingers

they glide and strum across your body to make a
remarkable noise and poised to play 'til daybreak

(like baptism by sunrise)

by dawn, a new name
to honor this song

<u>Wolf</u>

kiss her under a full moon
and she will growl
and try not to bite you

Ghost

I stare at him because he is powerful and I wonder if he
knows how beautiful that is: to be both humble and strong
arrogance as flippant as waving his hand at the bartender
to bring him another round while in the middle of telling a
funny story

When I look away from him, it's because I think he can tell
that his power is captivating
this quiet audacity in everything that he does is soothing
Not many that are born protectors take on their role

I don't fear love, but man is terrifying
Man is human while the soul is willed to love,
willed to acquiescence with any form given

What doesn't make us whole will make us wander

When we talk, I hold the collar of my shirt up a little past
my chin

I kiss him with my eyes closed

Frightened and elated all at once

Bluefish

the salt on his skin tastes like the ocean at low tide
like a meal on my tongue, my lips purse to cool
but he's always too hot
don't matter how hard I blow
I always drop him
and gotta pray on the five second rule

Nikki G. on the Boy

Listen to me tell you how to love me and I'll watch you
scream until you drown out the sound of my instructions
I've heard you call me a drill sergeant
But baby, I call you my soldier.
These are not commands.
These are orders.
Cause I just want to be specific.
Listen to me tell you how to love me.
If you hear me.
You won't complain.

You Know

she says, "I love you" and he doesn't say it back.
instead, he grabs her by the waist and pulls her close to
him.
kisses her neck, licks down to her shoulder
breathes in her ear like a lullaby; moves to spread her legs
like the wings of a butterfly,
heart to heart
she says, "I love you"
he doesn't say it back
they are connected
their hands, above her head, pressed so hard the knuckles
are white
their skin so wet, they are drinking each other
their intentions so intense that they cum together
like they've come together
he is holding her
her eyes are trying to close but her fears won't let it rest
she whispers, almost to herself
"why you don't never tell me you love me"
he tells her to look at him.
and when she does
he kisses every single tear
and he tells her, "because you know"

No Name Rapsody

Why they ain't give it to Eve?
Disrespect the Crown, got Laila fighting to dream
Cause they never understand how to respect all Queens
Say the ugliest things
About the sisters these days
Disregard our whole existence to give another one praise
Maybe I ain't so cute
Maybe I shouldn't smoke
Maybe they only think you righteous when you rocking a
fro
Maybe my sex ain't the best
Maybe this shit all a test
I ain't the one to study so better bet Imma guess
That's why Afeni in hiding
ain't no one to confide in
Say a real thing and they gone respond with the lying
B like "turn yaself in,
When you get out,
We'll head up to Paris"
But I know you tryna dim my muthafuckin light, put my
spirit in hiding
Doing shows in the closet
Most of us don't know nothing but fighting
It feels like we never got the right so I be cryin' and
writin'.

Taz

When the words you are avoiding are making
your fingers ache…

Poem

the poem about you
sleeps in my throat and snores like a dragon all day
daring me
to release the story of us
like fire from my lips
burning through my teeth and face
my breath scorched
the taste of you
like charred meat, fallen from bone
like home and holiday and hero
left to trace you
in the ashes
for the non-believers
who don't just drink anybody's tea
for the ones
who gotta see who's pouring the sugar

If only I could write of you in grain
bear down so hard on paper
we turn into dust
would the rain kneading into us
make us rise?
would I risk that?
Rather I swallow fire daily

my heart doused in burns.

Fabergé Eyes

"I ain't lying"
his eyes used to twinkle
like Sinatra had a single called 'Let There Be Light'
gave me butterflies

He blinked the blues.

Ski Mask Way

Beat my fist into walls that powdered my palms and hurt my
feelings
Like, "bitch you can't beat nobody"
Some shit don't knock down

I want to check on you.
I want to ask you if you are okay.
I want to ask you how work was today. How are your
parents, and your sisters and the dogs.

I want to ask, how close are you to the position you needed to
be in to commit to us?
I want to ask you were they worth it?
Specifically, those shes?
Those streets?
I want to ask you if you're writing?
Specifically, what's the piece?
I want to ask why me?
I want to ask how, me?

I stared at your image the other night.
I am stuck in stage anger.
love won't heal until I grieve.
Held together by spit and faith,
Dismantled by ugly truth and grease.
I can hear you saying what "y'all" taught you, from the screen.
I want to ask can you hear me grind my teeth?
Shit makes my ears bleed.

Still

We have not outgrown each other
Some nights
That tortures every part of my being

Rebirth of Slick

Like the echo of something passionate could keep me still

I find myself stuck to the memory like lint on a black shirt

All the cool gone. The Fonz would have my neck.

Lie spent on pillows with aches in my back from a day last week

I wonder if you feel me on your bones?

Genie

Run up
say some shit that moves me,
take me by the wrists and make your fingers make my
fingers grip you
you
make me move, some shit you say
run up
take me
by the risks, I'm sure this what I want
Why you hide?
Why I lie?
Maybe, I'll pop my knuckles and you appear

Love Letter

Resurrect me from shards of E flat
Lay me down on a chord that struck a nerve connected to
your heart
Part my lips and blow a lullaby inside
Let them pray
Ashes to notes
Quotes to dust

Hide and Seek

The oddness in the sky matched the color of the hickies on
my side.
I think the rain owes me a kiss on my mouth and the
world only belongs to lovers
and healers
I think power lies in the eyes of its beholders and beauty is
as beauty does and is all will ever be when you are either
lonely or in love or in love and in love
But they will explain away circumstance and I will find
another way to keep myself from him
'Cause love how we love doesn't fix with proclamation
More like threats and crocodile tears
But we mean it
Always have
We rehash as if yesterday is still between the teeth,
My legs
Or this linen
You have never been here, but I wanted you to be,
Does that count for something?
Love how we love is
A-typical, not typical, not in type, not always reciprocal, a
mental hieroglyphic, a glitch with a kill switch
Love how we love can't be explained, contained. I've tried
and I don't want to but maybe I do love you like you need
me to. Maybe you love me like I want you to. We just
don't know what that would feel like
Love how we love could last forever or ten minutes. The
length of an argument with no end

I give up on you
You have no patience with me
Love how we love
Is quiet at dusk and war at 3
a.m. to be specific it don't matter the time
A strike of pink the skyline reminds me of your tongue
outlining my flesh
The rain bouncing off of the wet asphalt sounds like an
invitation to get my face wet
The moon is screaming for me to count to ten.
But I cannot play with how I love him.

(24 Hour Mixtape)

I don't appreciate the invasiveness of my dreams.

Like, I would want to love him in my sleep.

Like, I'm not escaping the thought that I love him in every waking moment.

Like, I don't want to sleep it away.

So,

It's blunt rides and stolen highs until I can lie still at night

And sleep

Maybe

dream again.

<u>There</u>

caught in my throat
underneath my nails
on the bottom of my foot
I still feel you

like feline to catnip, the study of my skin his new pastime

an almost subtle commotion
in his frenzied fixation
will break his neck
to indulge this hobby

my body
returns to
elixirs
emulsified
melting
into something edible
delicious arrangement
like cbd oil and repent,
something vicious

I still feel you

and this is
just the beginning
just reliving the inner reeling
of you kissing
me

Lurkin'

the story will bury itself inside of her voice and she will
turn into one of them bitches that always sounds mad
glad he gone
but we talk about him like yesterday, she has tried to pray
away the word vomit, but his name slips out, in a rush,
like calling earl, after a night on her lush shit
but fuck it
she drunk and this is the last time
now she tries to scroll past his picture fast on her timeline
there's a new 'her' on his right side, and she thinks, again.
Like so many other times
I bet this time he gets it right
They always seem to see the light after you
But it's cool
Now she plays creep to niggas who sneak around on their
girls and wives,
The thinking?
She gotta keep him. He ain't mine.
But there's never no company for her at sunrise

The Blackberry Domino

Taz

she sits somewhere believing in you
and because I did too
her opinion won't change

A Requiem for the Routine

The day after always begins the same

It starts with me glowing in the face, smiling shyly, and
holding questions on my teeth.

Questions that go down the drain with the toothpaste.
I kiss you goodbye.

You don't open your eyes. I imagine that means either you
can't stand to watch me leave or it is you know that I will be
back.

One last trace of your face and I leave knowing that you
won't be home when I get back.

This day always ends the same

I shower and remember.
I lie in bed and search for answers to questions that I've
never asked you.
I wake up under a full moon only to realize my sheets are
wet, the day is gone and you are not here.
But I knew that you wouldn't be here.

Sweat and tears make the linens salty and prove that
wisdom is fragile.
Headaches and an empty stomach remind me that

Taz

knowledge hurts
And I
Will never understand what wills my fate but that my faith
in love is unwavering.

Predestined and still, I believe in you.

Enter the Woo

He is smooth complexion, like never seen a pimple, bright
eyes like moon rise and dimples
He is big laugh and deep voice he is rose from the concrete
a gangsta and a gentleman, a super thug and American,
gangster, a dirty red turned X,
He is a vex on my conscience
He doesn't always take his ring off.
Don't really give me no options

Smokey

He was not who he wanted to be.
No previous example of a father figure: his father figured
it was better the boy thought he was an uncle. And that
his stepfather was the daddy.
Didn't gladly hand over his rights. Just the boys mama
won't his wife.
And his wife loves him.
His kids love him.
This woman does, too. Loves her freedom more though.
Still, she gave that lover her all.
And that boy. Man, he loves his uncle.
Always wanted to ride with that uncle, get a haircut with
that uncle. Listen to music, watch football with that uncle.
His mama couldn't stand it.
The damage couldn't be reversed when the boy's uncle
died from agent Orange.
Insurance agents came in with papers.
Say, "Well, his uncle left him some money."
He wanted the boy to know his father always loved him.

Fast forward.

This boy grows into a hardworking man.
A provider. Got that from watching his mother.
And from watching his mother he loved ambitious
women. Beautiful women.
But the other side was infatuated with the deserving, the
hard working.

So he's married to a model.
His heart belongs to a waitress.
His first taste of love bore his legacy and he still replaced it.
Chose his mother, maybe?
Emotional matrix.
He and she are his mother and father right now.
He and she are his mother and father right now.
She makes him wonder how his mama's husband feels.
So he argues with the past to be allowed to raise the future.
And he argues with the present to just be a gift.
But when he argues with now, it's always about time.
Cause maybe he can forget about the present and the past.
Maybe he can forget about his mother and father and dad.
Maybe he can feel like a grown up with all of his big things
Maybe he can get on her level and just step on his shoe strings.
Scream some E.P.M.D.
Dance and laugh and Be!
She once cried into his chest that she wished he was free.
That waitress did.
And he could only lie to her that one day he would be.
Now became later. And never came back.
He knows who his father was. What his mama did and what his daddy put up with.
What he doesn't know is why he isn't angry with his mother.
So he stays.
That's what she did. Right?

Debbie and Craig

I want to say his name out loud.
I want to hold his hand in a crowded elevator and rub the
sleep out of his eye with my spit, like I'm sure his wife
does.
He asks me what I think of.
I lie and say him
But I lie in bed at night and think about her fucking him.
How lucky she is.
I think about how I am on call.
I think about bucking.
I never do.
Doctor's never do.
Florence Nightingale to his need.
I pretend, is of me.
You can't sweat out adultery
Insurance don't cover this sickness
I wonder if I am killing him
Maybe I want to
Die old maid in a shoe to take care of him,
Pictures of his family vacation make me look at pearls and
Pina coladas differently
She looks like a Mannequin
He looks like the preacher
I feel like that first lady on some shit
Like I don't know my hem too high
I don't ask because you don't let their names come out
your mouth
Mental rule

But I wonder
He asks bout mine
I tell him everything
Us bitches ain't got no respect
Better yet
We don't got nobody to talk to
I want to say his name out loud.
I call him my boyfriend.
There is nothing worth mentioning about how he treats
me.

Deebo

I want to ask his wife
if it's alright
if her husband just stayed the night.
It seems to me
the remedy to this insanity we coexist in.
In his hand. I am not the Queen
I've always been the joke and to her just a Jezebel.
Fiendish to say his name out loud
Just want to hold his hand next to a wishing well and
dance with him in a crowd
I think about how I am on call for him.
Florence Nightingale to his need.
And I pretend he needs me. But you can't sweat out
adultery
Insurance don't cover this sickness
I wonder if I am killing him
Maybe I want to
Die old maid in a shoe to take care of him,
Pictures of his family vacation make me look at pearls and
Pina coladas differently
She looks like a Mannequin
He looks like the preacher
I feel like that first lady who sits in the front row acting
like she don't know her hem too high and neither does she
mind
Why won't you let him spend the night?
So you can boast about the 14th of February and the 25th
of December cause you know where he won't be.

Like that accounts for
The day before or the day after
We both remember
Now Tell me
It doesn't eat at you
That faraway look at the dinner table
It's never a meal for two
If y'all the perfect gumbo I'm the fly in the soup
The reason he ain't posting about you
And the reason sometimes he do
He will not leave you
He will not disappoint you
But you are not the only woman he cares about
He loves your kids
But he loves ours too
And It that I ain't got no respect
Better yet
A bitch don't got nobody to talk to
So will you
Let him spend the night?

Witches Brew

The way the wind swirls underneath the leaves, I know
that demons dance
Found sweaty in a boiler room full of magicians
Not a single regret here
Just every now and then a joke about how they do it on
the other side

Ain't I, Ain't I

Ain't I a woman?
A masterpiece inside of a mess.
A puddle before the rain
Walking ocean
Sleeping earth
Ain't I a woman?
Hard working and bold
Ain't I sexy and fearless?
Ain't I a liar and a serpent?
Like you didn't eat the apple cause you was hungry too?
Ain't I the moon?
My walk like wave
Touch out of space?
I see the stars in your eyes when you stare at me
Look at me
Alien
You see one but there's two
Full womb
Fire breather
Life Bearer
Man eater
Meteor
This child be a comet
The center of my Universe
You be the Sun
The lighting for the show
Ain't I a woman?
Taking credit for the whole shit.

Taz

Shoving your nose in it.
As if I am training you.
As if I am taming you.
I'd go mad to be stripped of my free
You'd be glad to be done and rid of me
Like I ain't your woman
Your rib
Your reflection
Your better half
Like I ain't your woman
Your saltwater
Your fresh air
Your healer
Like I ain't your woman
Your baby mother
Your lover
Your best friend
Like I ain't your wife
Like this ain't your life
Like
A million similes are necessary to describe
You and I
You are mine
This man
Ain't I
your woman?

Double Dutch

If she loved you, she loves you
There's no denying that
Split this fact like two ropes
With her body in the middle
Jumping up and down to this rhythm
A heartbeat that rocks you when you see her
Like, nigga was that a thump?

Sitting at the Back Table
– CIPHERTuesdays Open Mic

I wanna stay
But the way this other man looked at me today
It struck me to my core
I wanna stay
Lay down groundwork for a future impossible, every
obstacle worth the years, the time
I wanna stay
But the way this other man looked at me today it struck
me to my core
His eyes floated to mine like a butterfly rising from the
battlefields of war
Like two steady bullets destined to me the target, shot
through my retinas, detonated inside of my pupils
He was beautiful, rueful, an eye full a spoonful
A stare held, an image burned, a crux imagined and
realized
Can you be penalized for fornication in seconds
It touched me
So, I hope not
I want to stay
Maybe the tide hasn't shifted, the ocean has changed
The difference between tsunami and hurricane
My lashes fell wet, blinking
I want to stay
With my eyes closed
Where I can see him
And he is closer

And bolder and I am stronger, and we are wires and this
current is sustaining us
The only thing containing us here
Like Jill say
I think it's better that I tell you know

<u>Choke</u>

She tired of crying
so she scream his name and let him fuck tears from her
eyes

People can be like petals
Beautiful, then fall off for no other reason but time

The Alpha & Omega

Their bodies collapse in a way that justifies weak
foundations

The rubble more beautiful than the view of them standing

The destruction more deeply felt than the blueprint

They have started at the end.
All that is left is the beginning.

Rollover to Voicemail

I could pretend it doesn't bother me, but it would continue
to bother me. It bothers me
Am I'm not supposed to feel that?
Not supposed to be warranted.
I'm killing the vibe?
Taz?
Yeah, right.
I could be fuckin in a cheap motel getting high right now ,
But tomorrow would come.
Life so strange

Left on Read

Find myself restless, hanging on to the edge of every
affection, only partially wanting its presence but wholly
wanting
to touch
and to feel
its warmth
sincerity not as optional as it had once been..
I do not know if this is sadness
or just indecision with playing along with the bullshit

All of It

The images, the words, the notions begin to blur earlier in the day than I admit to but I pretend that it is all pristine in the moment.
I pretend the inflections don't matter.
But they do.

Cheshire Moon

the waning moon broke out in a smile

rose up by an undercurrent of power, fostered by the wind

(or sweet sorrow)

like someone smushed my face in it, I wipe the craters out
of my eyes.

stars lie on my lashes wet enough to make it
seem as if I'm crying.

I probably was.

but all will be forgotten,
forgiven

by morning

I'm a Good Person
(Standing RSVP)

I mean,
if you asked me to try on wedding dresses I would. I
mean, for like pretend. For you
if you wanna know if I wanna watch wedding proposals
on YouTube, I do. Especially the white folks dammit.
(Chet be showing out.)
Like, if someone asked, you have to have like a white
lemon cake, so people don't get dirty...or whatever. If it
were me. But it's not.
And I mean, don't invite me to your shit, cause I wanna
go. But I'm not gonna go.
Cause I'll be crying for me
And you'll think I'm happy for you
And I'm just a better bitch than that.

<u>Seasons' Change</u>

the cadence of passion rumbles underneath the belly, like
a cramp crippling your walk..
stand upright and pretend you don't love anything
anymore or ever did
like brittle leaves don't make you sad because you are so
grateful for autumn.
You don't miss the color green
You don't miss the heat
You enjoy the fall as a reminder that things have changed
The air has switched
And time won't pause if you buckle.

Loch Ness Monster

his eyes pierce like arrows through bulls' eyes
find myself an easy target, heartbeat a spotlight
find myself hiding in plain view
I have to watch
I wonder if he really sees me or
is that just the look of a warrior turned pirate
make me talk like a sailor to myself
go overboard and wonder if he'll anchor
cast away first nature
do not think of drowning
only think of the surrounding water
pressure
surrender
a death that pleads for sanctuary
muddled professions gurgling through saltwater and dirt
like you knew I'd die for you

<u>Scotch</u>

Voice breaks in a bend of air that can't carry sound
A jet noise of wind drowning out the crack
So, he kissed me on my tears
Tasted the sadness he couldn't hear
Drank goodbye and turned his back

Red Carpet

The clacking of her 3-inch gel tipped nails on the marble
kitchen table sounded like expensive annoyance
like the peasantry of the situation distorted the reality of
the situation.

She too good for him.

The chamber of her .22 filled to the brim with regrets and
contempt, hellbent on suppression behind her manicured
finger. But this nigga really taking too long to get in the
house.

A spouse with no couth is like a single bitch with no class:
trash.

The trailer of her life flashes before her eyes
counterclockwise. La cinema on her wrist. She twitches at
the suspense.

His 6 series pulls into the driveway and he shuts the
engine off.

She wonders if he is thinking of her.

(She wonders if he is thinking of her.)

The keys gently clang against the door and as it opens, she
shoots.

She rose from her chair slowly. The kickback from the minor explosion was giving her more fan hair than Beyonce.

The splatter of his insides strewn like roses on the red carpet.
The thud of his lifeless body sounded like a compressed round of applause from a paparazzi of one.

And, for once, this nigga gave her a show.

They have a tendency to spiral

"Nah"

– Rosa Parks

Nah
This ain't a poem about corona
This is a poem about another corner
Another coroner
And another cop
Another set of riots
And some plots to win elections
By saving some hoes
Who don't need to be saved
Because they'd rather be heard
Than herded
On a land where the brave been knew that
Don't confuse that
the backs refuse to break
by God's grace
from sea to shining sea
Lord forbid we
lose a Target, a Honda or an ABC
Some shit is essential
Like teachers
Heal the virus with home schooling
Credentials not needed
Just heated debate
And plastered smiles
Glory be to the aisles and aisles
Of toilet paper
Lord, may joy come in the morning under lavender sky

Where Black mate doesn't look other race mate in the eye
And have to ask them if they'll ride
When the flames rise
To burn the swine
They in the bread basket with the biscuits buttered
The words being mumbled sound like redemption song
Call it more like a rumble, a hymn in song
Somebody still dreaming that we will overcome
Oppression
Depression
Desperation
The vacant look in the eyes of a youth that don't know
what's going on
But they can see the future
And fully commit to the shits
Fuck it, take the masks off
This ain't a poem about corona
Might don't even be a poem about the corner , the coroner,
or the cop
This ain't about the leaders we need
Or the ones we forgot
This ain't about the riots the resistance fighters
or the cities on fire

How many of our children have seen a man die?
In real time.
How many haven't seen a so called slave movie, or
studied a man named Huey, but will indubitably die for
the cause?
This time it's hashtag George Floyd
Two weeks ago hashtag Ahmaud

The list literally goes on and on
I myself have written poems
For Korryn
Sandra
And Trayvon
These cousins
So I call them by first name
Claim them in chain letter
To Senators who don't forward
Still I'll sign another petition
Watch friends kneel at partitions
Dividing state and fate
Dividing race and faith
Dividing anger and hate
Where's the love?
I took the gloves off, cause this is not a poem about corona
Do not confuse pandemic and genocide
50 million people died during smallpox in the 50s
6 million died during the Holocaust.
Or rather we compare Black Plague and Transatlantic
trade
How much that dollar cost?
Respect the depth of a single death and its debt
forget smudging the numbers
Rest assured
This is not a poem about corona
Just feels the same
Cause the temperature ain't changed
And I don't know if there is a cure.

Taz

An Ode to Panic

I'm not scared

But every weekend

We clean the house

From top to bottom

(only the people that be here)

We run errands in our masks

And raw dog the wind on 7/11 runs

risking it all

Today

I'm supposed to be writing about the coronavirus,
highlight this pandemic
this time in history
where we're quarantined
because breathing the air
too deeply
in these streets
could get you killed.

I'm supposed to be writing about Nip and Kobe
and how if only they
were still
living
black boys around the world wouldn't feel like
a piece of their hearts are missing
wouldn't feel like every dream worth wishing
doesn't turn into
a fallen star

I'm supposed to be writing about my mentor who died
that I just realized, the year prior, had become one of my
best friends
and how that makes me feel.
eulogizing someone who is alive in my heart.
and how that makes me feel.

I'm supposed to be writing
about unrequited love,

Taz

the never ending madness of loyalty
and the craving for what should have been,
in a grain that lets you know that pain has been slow to
heal
and I've tried
but I can't contrive
words to reach
the depth of each
grief
as if poetry
doesn't suffer
it's fair share
of misery
every time
we decide
to speak on
the things we know
there are no words for

ignoring the strawberry bruises
each reasoning daily leaves behind
to bear new fruit

because I'm supposed to be writing

<u>Without Rosary</u>

Gather round the toilet paper and ammunition, hold
hands and let us bow our heads
pray God that the Wi-Fi doesn't go out
and that the Saints may take communion everyday
including Sunday
it's essential that we partake

The Last First Day

The night Tonie Morrison died, Janis Joplin asked her
for a dance
They talked about Vietnam all night
Reminisced on Woodstock and the Bluest Eye
Nelson Mandela and John Lennon
You know
Just what it was like when their souls hit the air
Jan whispered bout how she fucked a Black man who had
ducked the war
And Tonie whispered about how she loved men who
could never be a representation of her people
You know, the things we women talk about over playing
cards or sipping tea
Behind closed doors and kitchen sinks; yo that's just that
on that
When revolution could be questioned
Because we believed everything we had been taught
was a lie
Or at least not science
When everything was God
And we could challenge that nigga cause we ain't seen him
Too many of us don't know our daddy's
Too many of us don't claim our feelings
So God became needles
Or basketballs
Or pens
And the only way you see heaven is if you kill yourself
practicing for Coachella or if you almost freeze standing in

30 degrees
Beyoncé, my weed man, and poets is angels
In heaven
I imagine the black people mingle and talk shit
Like Malcom X sitting with the Kennedys over an Irish
breakfast and a Muslim fast
Or like Capone facing Warhol for a painting while he
snickers that the fruit cup better not paint him as a soup can
Basquiat chuckles he would never, plus it'd make his
momma mad
Respect got layers
But the truth is the truth
The universe blesses us with examples
We tend to call them legends
Or ancestors
We tend to call them monsters
Or lost
We tend to call them genius
With demons
We tend to call them everything but what their mamas
called them like if I had prolific tatted on my face you'd
gun me down like I ain't human
Am I too prolific to be human?
Will they shoot me off my podium
Will I die unrecognized
I'm not ashamed to say their names
Will they lift mine?
Want to be worthy of sitting between Eartha Kitt and
Afeni in heaven
ask them what bravery be about
I wanna know why Marvin wasn't on Ooooh Child, but at

least once a week I play inner city blues on an Old Town
road
And
Wait
For
The
Beat
To
Drop
'Cause that's when everything gets a little bit easier
Forgiveness is a virtue
Feel like I've been living in my church shoes a muse for
failure and God
I fear failure and God
I fear not being forgiven by those I love and being ripped
of my vocal chords
Or the ability of my fingers to move
. The night Tonie died, Janis asked her for a dance
Janis told her not to cry
To just wipe her eyes and dance, furiously
Because dying doesn't have to be hard even if it is
And Alice is holding up her Walker under a purple sky
waiting for them to drop blood on the dance floor of an
awkward wonderland
So they danced
And they danced
By the end of the song they were both screaming In
paradigm
Creation on its last breath
I think I heard it

Bitches is Me

Yo.
I got tired one day
Shit.
I didn't even want the free meal, the plug or the 40 dollars
The fake ass hollers,
The "Oh ma lemme talk to you"
You looking good
Lemme walk with you
Is This your hood?
I got no response
For real, I'm tired
Don't want no dick pics, no eggplant emojis, or no heart
eyes, no video chats and texts filled with lies, all the
feelings contrived, broadcasted live.
Some shit you done sent 50 chicks up and down the
timeline
don't write me no poems no songs
Ion mean no harm
I'm tired
Retired
I'm tryna be a unicorn
An unpeeled orange
A muthafuckin pink starburst
I've already rehearsed my welcome back speech into
virginity
It goes Simply
I'm just happy to be here
Thank y'all for having me

Grateful to be forgiven of all my casualties at this here gate
If that's what it takes
Cause I know I been playing
But I'm saying
It was like
One day,
I just got tired. Knew the vibration between he and I
couldn't go no higher, didn't feel no fire, like flat
rubber tires with the slow leak, there was no peep but you
could hear it
The ending, like stop signs at both aortas, no intersection
in our intestines
Our stomachs weren't in knots,
No butterflies
more like kidneys filled with rocks, dialysis couldn't keep
us alive
The Shit was tired
Never-ending and over, bent and sober, like a callous on a
pretty foot still needs hiding
So, I'm deciding to wait on my prince charming and I
know fairytales are dying at an alarming rate
But if ya boy believes that that's her body
And ya girl swears on her husband's faith
Then slide me to the side like Nipsey mama and
Let me do my thing
Please
Cause I'm just tired
But I wanna believe
Wear my heart on my sleeve like black label
Hope it burst into colors, like my old favorite shirt
Make me forget my old favorite hurt

Be everything it's worth
A possibility
Or I ain't gonna be able to do it
Won't be no getting Lucky
Niggas get shot down every day
Just leave me, B
Cant u hear it?
Don't u see?
Bitches is tired.
It's me.
I'm Bitches, bitches is me.

Blackberry Domino

In a season where the black boys are dying in record
numbers and the mothers fall ill to surviving,
there will be daughters who plan to become millionaires
and take care of their parents and nana
There will be sons who step in as fathers to children who
will never know theirs just as they had never known their
own
There will be sisters who define the true nature of running
water and bad blood
Moon talk disregarded as gibberish
Like the universe made it up
And I laugh because there are too many stars in my belly
not to,
Too many sunrises in my cheeks and nighttimes in my
eyes
The world is in me
I know my body
In a season where love isn't hobby
Where I won't let them try me no matter how lonely the
dawns be
God been watching
somehow needs me to do better
Proclaiming the sons name after 2 am ain't cutting it
Needs me to shout for Jesus in the day time
With my eyes open
And my palms crossed and dry
I think I've been to the outskirts of heaven in lucid dreams
and indulgent highs , I'm sure it will have me

Flaws and all
I know how to talk to angels
And demons
They might make me security at the gates
I told y'all purgatory won't gonna suck for me
In a season where I may finally shed skin
More than tears
In a season where I only fear my heart.
In a season where I only trust my heart.

21

I watched the afternoon sky shift to purple while exhaling
moon rocks over a chest built from black ice and stars.
Met Oblivion with the sun in my eyes and stripes across
my throat.
Sweating bullets in God's lap , lapping up the sins up with
a silver tongue
A snow storm fills a barren cave with hope, the way that
diamonds tend to do
Hope I do not melt and evaporate back into the universe
It is the longest night of the year and we plan to mine 'til
daybreak

Can't Take My Joy

If you catch me at the end of the world, touching the sky
and the water and God

With the moon shining on my skin and the wind
whispering in my ears

Know that I am happy here
Full and free
Quiet
Feeling no regret

In a space, where the end is a blur
A place they call horizon

Or Zion
To those who know

<u>Dive</u>

at the edge of nowhere I hurled my body off the cliff
outstretched my arms and instantaneously began to crash
broke every bone in my body and died with my eyes wide
open
and a smile on my face wider than a Cheshire grin
if reincarnation exists
this moment my birthright
I was born to begin again

colophon
Brought to you by Wider Perspectives Publishing, care of James Wilson, with the mission of advancing the poetry and creative community of Hampton Roads, Virginia.

See our production of works from ...

Edith Blake
Tanya Cunningham-Jones
     (Scientific Eve)
Terra Leigh
Ray Simmons
Samantha Borders-Shoemaker
Bobby K.
     (The Poor Man's Poet)
J. Scott Wilson (TEECH!)
Charles Wilson
Gloria Darlene Mann
Neil Spirtas
Zach Crowe
Jorge Mendez & JT Williams
Sarah Eileen Williams
Stephanie Diana (Noftz)
the Hampton Roads
     Artistic Collective
Jason Brown (Drk Mtr)
Martina Champion

Tony Broadway
Ken Sutton
Crickyt J. Expression
Lisa M. Kendrick
Cassandra IsFree
Nich (Nicholis Williams)
Samantha Geovjian Clarke
Natalie Morison-Uzzle
Gus Woodward II
Patsy Bickerstaff
Catherine TL Hodges
Jack Cassada
Dezz
Chichi Iwuorie

... and others to come soon.

We promote and support the artists of the 757
from the seats, from the stands,
from the snapping fingers and
clapping hands
from the pages, and the stages
and now we pass them forth
to the ages

Check for the above artists on FaceBook, the Virginia Poetry Online channel on YouTube, and other social media.

Hampton Roads Artistic Collective is charitable extension of WPP which strives to simultaneously support worthy causes in Hampton Roads and the local creative artists.

www.ingramcontent.com/pod-product-compliance
Lightning Source LLC
Chambersburg PA
CBHW072255270326
41930CB00010B/2386